SOARING ON THE WIND

Blanik thermal soaring just off Torrey Pines, California. GEORGE UVEGES

JOSEPH COLVILLE LINCOLN

SOARING ON THE WIND

A photographic essay on silent flight

 NORTHLAND PRESS

Other books by
Joseph Colville Lincoln

SOARING FOR DIAMONDS

ON QUIET WINGS

To Lloyd and Rose Marie Licher

I watched him strap on his harness and helmet,
climb into the cockpit and, minutes later, a black dot, fall
off the wing two thousand feet above our field.
At almost the same instant, a white streak behind him
flowered out into the delicate, wavering muslin
of a parachute — a few gossamer yards grasping onto
air and suspending below them, with invisible
threads, a human life, a man who by stitches, cloth,
and cord, had made himself a god of the sky
for those immortal moments.

A day or two later, when I decided that I too must pass
through the experience of a parachute jump, life rose
to a higher level, to a sort of exhilarated calmness. The
thought of crawling out onto the wing, through a
hurricane of wind, clinging on to struts and wires
hundreds of feet above the earth, and then giving up
even that tenuous hold of safety and of substance, left
in me a feeling of anticipation mixed with dread, of
confidence restrained by caution, of courage salted
through with fear. How tightly should one hold on to
life? How loosely give it rein? What gain was there
for such a risk? I would have to pay in money for hurling
my body into space. There would be no crowd to
watch and applaud my landing. Nor was there any
scientific objective to be gained. No, there was a deeper
reason for wanting to jump, a desire I could not
explain. It was the quality that led me into aviation
in the first place — it was a love of the air and sky
and flying, the lure of adventure, the appreciation of
beauty. It lay beyond the descriptive words of men
— where immortality is touched through danger, where
life meets death on equal plane; where man is more
than man, and existence both supreme and valueless
at the same instant.

CHARLES A. LINDBERGH

Every soaring pilot
builds his own treasure house
of memories.

It might begin when he first sees a gaggle of sailplanes turning in a thermal, over a nearby field on a warm summer day. The flight motion is surprisingly slow; to an eye on the ground it has the strange formality of an eighteenth century court dance, performed at half pace. The slender-winged ships turn round and round, but they do not sink toward the earth. Perceptibly they rise in the air — without power, without a sound except for an occasional delicate whistle that comes and goes on the air.

The rise of the sailplanes is readily explained to the mind — but the mind is only one part of life. Seeing it through the more elemental comprehension of the belly or the bones, there is feeling that a miracle is taking place: the law of gravity is being put aside. And in all of it — the warmth of the quiet day, the sudden rush of air into a thermal or dust devil, the yearning thrust of cumulus clouds overhead, and in the shape and motion of the turning sailplanes, there is a disturbing loveliness which can never be quite forgotten.

Surprises come tumbling during the first soaring lesson. There is unearthly strangeness in the early transition training flights to a pilot long schooled in power flying — no propeller, no engine instruments, no engine noise or vibration, the stomach turning queasy from minute after minute of tight circling in bumpy air. When you were a student the other time, your instructor kept saying, "You don't really move the stick, just put pressure on it," this to keep you from horsing the airplane all over the sky with overcontrol. Now, flying in rough thermals just above stall, there are full control deflections and always, from the back seat, the instructor hammering at you with a steady stream of unflattering orders.

The first landings! Approaching the field, getting lower, determined to start downwind from the right altitude, the field close, then the impossible compression of requirements: right altitude, the right airspeed, coordination, the right distance to the side of the runway to make room for a solid base leg, the right altitude for turning onto base, the lower altitude for turning final, and in your throat the nearly-shouted but always unspoken question: What if we have to go around again?

The short flights, recorded in the logbook with an abbreviated notation and the instructor's initials and commercial license number:

> *To & La* (Takeoff and landing), *Turns, 15 minutes*
> *To & La, Turns, 20 minutes*
> *To & La, Turns, Stalls, 1 hr. 10 min.*
> *"SOLO" 1 hr. and 20 min.*
> *Solo. To & La. 15 min.*

"I'm going with you this time," he says.

Why? You wonder. Wasn't that last landing all right? He didn't say anything about it. There was no groundloop on touchdown. Both altitude and speed had been very close to right on downwind, base leg and final. Maybe not enough allowance for the wind which had picked up.

Anyway, back into the ship for a dual ride, the exalted feeling of independence lost. Seatbelt and shoulder harness on, canopy down and locked, towline hooked up. The tow begins. We take off, cross the far border of the field and make a shallow turn left, climbing steadily. There is no instruction from the back seat, just unnerving silence. *What did I do wrong?*

An instant crack as from a light rifle: "Towline break — what are you going to do?" he shouts.

Quickly now, a 180-degree turn with the nose well down to keep up good speed — there we are, heading back toward the field, everything under control. . . .

"You shouldn't fly right over the field, set up a landing pattern, either on this side or the other."

A half-right turn for a long downwind leg — keep it in fairly close, no room to spare this time — there, a little beyond the downwind end, turn base . . . now final . . . a trace of spoiler. Now, put it on . . . gently.

Check sim. towline break, 5 minutes, he notes in his logbook.

More solo flights, the next one an hour and a half, up to 5600 feet above terrain, feeling comfortable in the ship, at home except for the backache problem which comes after the first hour. Next week a 30-minute flight up to 3500 feet above terrain, then heavy sink and a dash back to the field. Another tow — this time finding very strong lift in three thermals and soaring up to 13,100 above terrain, 14,500 feet above sea level for a club altitude record. Coming back two hours later, shivering; then the landing and talking it over, face stiff with cold, speech difficult as if your mouth were covered with a heavy glove.

Next week the lift failed on a brief solo flight. I tried to find it over a knoll which was an exceptionally good spot — nothing; then over a more distant ridge — nothing; finally in a patch of dry wash in the Salt River bed — stable air. Only 800 feet left now. *This is it.* Not a prayer of getting back without lift, and I haven't hit a bump since release. Don't panic. That place up ahead looks good for landing — flat, smooth, just low bushes to watch for — might even be able to aerotow out of it. Then fly over to it and get a closer look . . . still looks good. Thank God. No other place is possible now. 600 feet left. Over 270 degrees to turn. You aren't anywhere near the right place to start the downwind leg of your pattern. Don't panic. Oh God, for some lift. From 500 feet? Keep that nose down. What do you mean keep the nose down? You've got nearly 70 airspeed. 450 feet — roll into downwind — straighten out — watch those trees ahead. We seem higher than 450. Naturally. The river bottom's lower than the field, you idiot. Speed O.K. I don't think my chest will quite burst. Not too far from the end of that good patch now, but don't turn too soon. 300 feet. NOW! Easy. That's it. Straighten out a little on base. 200 feet. Roll into final. Speed O.K. Less than 90 degrees to turn. Now straighten out again. Still 80 or 90 feet left. Field looks worse from this angle. Better a trace to the right. *Now's the time.* Slow down a little. A touch of spoiler. That's doing it. Spoiler off. Just a few feet high. Sound of the wheel touching bushes — now banging against hummocks of sand. Full brakes and spoilers. A series of wrenching bounces — the right wing goes down in the bushes, the sailplane ground-loops 80 degrees to the right, stops and rolls back a foot.

Everything O.K.? I guess I am. How about the ship? I undo the seat belt, shoulder harness, and take off the parachute, then get out and make a careful inspection of the LK. Not a scratch on it! Well! Not bad for a first emergency landing.

The field was of sand — too soft for an aerotow retrieve. The rest of the day was spent knocking down the sailplane and getting it on the trailer — then worrying the car and loaded trailer out to a narrow road, going back to nearby Falcon Field, rigging the sailplane again and putting it away for the night by which time it was after dark.

A break of a month, then the critical day for the flight test and a note in the log-book by the instructor. *Check ride for "Private" O.K.* D. Barnard CG 381000. I had made it.

Most of the early outlandings were on dirt roads, in sight of home base at Falcon Field, before cross-country days, when the spirit of adventure outreached the glide angle of a Baby Albatross. In a few minutes the gray Super-Cub towplane was in the air, on its way to retrieve. It circled overhead and landed nearby. The towrope was laid out and connected. Presently the Super-Cub wagged its rudder to ask if you were ready; you wagged yours to answer yes, then he gave it full throttle and immediately disappeared in a cloud of boiling dust. After a few seconds to accelerate, you were in it, the road barely visible, towline out of sight, but speed increasing, then the dust began thinning perceptibly and suddenly you were in the air.

Those early soaring days were when you competed in winter contests, after thermals were over for the season. The events were Spot Landing (where you tried to stop the nose of your ship as close as possible to a bright plastic cone on the runway), Bomb Drop (a sack full of sand was dropped over the side hoping it would hit a circular target on the ground marked with white powder), Altitude Gain (zero), Duration (the time needed to glide from release to landing at minimum sink), and the wonderful Ribbon Cutting event. The towpilot would throw a roll of toilet paper out of his ship just as you released. It quickly unrolled, leaving a vertical ribbon of paper about two hundred feet high, sinking through the air — you dove through it, cutting it with your wing, then made a vertical bank to reverse direction and cut it again, maneuvering violently, yelling at the top of your lungs in each turn to keep from blacking out from centrifugal force, until after six or eight cuts you were down to five hundred feet where it was required that you break off and set up a pattern for landing.

One of the earliest soaring friends was Bob Sparling of Prescott, always at the airport on weekends, wearing his baseball cap with the enormous long plastic bill, telling you what it was like to fly the 1947 National in his secondary. He is an old hand who worked in the era when they still made wooden ribs. The outer members, curved in airfoil shape, and the diagonals and risers were of light colored spruce, cheery in hue as captured sunlight. The little gussets were of dark laminated plywood, and the built-up ribs were fastened with glue and tiny golden brads made of brass.

When these were finished and placed on wooden spars, it was time for the covering. Fabric was cut, sewn and ribstitched, then the shop would smell of nitrate dope, brushed onto the fabric and shinking it over the ribs in graceful concave curves. After the first coat, fibers would stand up on the cover, the surface was sanded, then came another coat, another sanding, and still another coat, with fingers gradually becoming sore, until at last it was time for the silver dope and the color.

Another old hand was Ernie Schweizer, big, bald, heavy, honest, with a voice that has a friendliness and serenity unlike any other. He lives on Sing Sing Road in the village of Horseheads in a modest white house with shutters that have glider silhouettes cut out of them, but his real life is in the President's office at his factory, surrounded by drawers full of blueprints, a pipe always in his mouth, his hand always drawing sketches on a paper as he talks. For a long generation, soaring pilots have flown ships that he designed and built; one shining face of his monument will number those whose lives were saved by the mighty strength of his sailplanes.

The Schweizer factory at Elmira! There are sheets of aluminum, painted the brilliant chartreuse of zinc-chromate; racks of spar material coated dark olive green; production jigs made from arc-welded lengths of great steel pipe, and on them wings growing toward completion; 2–32 fuselages under construction, upside down, bristling with clecos. There is the petulant whine of air drills; the tommy gun staccato of rivet guns. In another room, the gentle, feminine hiss of an acetylene torch, its copper tip bent downward like a finger pointing at the lines of a page, the torch and welding rod expertly guided around clusters of steel tubing. An inch or two from the center the work is deep red, a color visible only at night, then it quickly brightens into cherry red, orange, yellow, and a searing white heat just under the hard, blue, cone-shaped flame.

Out behind the plant, separating it from the airport, is a lovely copse of pines, cool and quiet even in midsummer.

Who can remember all the days he has been aloft? And all the different sailplanes — each one loyal, each as individual as a person. The quiet of the 2–32 cockpit, so quiet you can hear the towplane's engine while you climb toward release altitude, watching the bright yarn yaw indicator snap in the wind, maneuvering your ship to keep the towrope taut. The gentle oilcanning sound of a 1–23D wing when you fly into a thermal, so emotionally welcome after the quiet of a long glide when you are low.

At altitude: Cold. Breathing requires a heavy pull of the lungs because of the Air Force A–13 mask, connected by an elephant trunk flexihose to its A–14 regulator, each breath indicated on the instrument panel by a faintly obscene wink of the oxygen blinker.

Flying in rough air. The wings flex nervously and streamers of blowing dust indicate rising surface wind. Fifteen minutes later the airspeed leaps from a stall to seventy miles per hour in a quarter of a turn. You get thrown around in the cockpit; a violent side gust hits the tailcone and makes a sound like the mournful note of a French horn. Drinking is impossible; the canteen would break teeth if used, and the stomach is in upheaval. You force yourself to eat little bits of bread, one cubic centimeter every ten minutes to keep from getting sick.

Times when the sky is in slumber, which you know during the performance testing flights at dawn, in cool air without bumps; climbing on tow thousands of feet high, the towplane quiet, not jumping around in front of you as it does on a good thermal day, the towrope in a gentle stationary sag — motion being seen but not felt as the earth goes by slowly, the altimeter showing steady climb, with a gentle swish from the passing air. Then release at the prearranged altitude, after a checking glance at your note pad, strapped onto a leg. You begin test runs, concentrating every fiber on keeping the yaw string centered, control movements tiny, and the airspeed exact, so the altimeter seems to be driven by the sweep second hand of your clock.

Torrey Pines. The takeoff area for winch tow with you parachuted, seated, and buckled into the Baby Albatross. It is a bright sunny day, but little wind is coming from the ocean. The starter comes over.

"Have you ever winch towed before?"

"No."

"Well, make sure you're off the wire before you turn."

"O.K."

"You'll accelerate and get airborne amazingly fast. Don't horse back on the stick until you have at least fifteen or twenty feet of altitude. Give yourself a chance to recover in case the cable breaks."

He goes back to the side. The wingtip is raised level; the flag drops — then explosive acceleration — you are airborne and climbing. A slack in the cable. Is it broken? Turn off to the right, *but release first*. O.K. About 200 feet above the runway, out over the cliff now. Sinking. . . . We weren't as high as I thought. No lift. Getting down to the cliff top. A 180-degree turn. Still sinking down the tan weathered earthen cliff — another turn, halfway down. Somebody up on top is motioning, but I can't look. The cliff, beach, ocean and sky. Getting lower. One last turn. It's going to be on the beach this time! Heading north toward the outcropping. Touchdown and landing roll. We stop and a wingtip settles to the wet sand.

Time? Three minutes in the air. This, after dreaming of setting a new duration record.

But there was another day, with a stiff wind rippling the Pacific, in another ship, a 1–23D, when the launch came in the blue-white light of forenoon, when it was easy to stay aloft even at that early hour and as time went on, you could climb 100, 200, then 500 feet above the cliff top, and from that altitude you could dive right down to the beach and zoom back to the top. You could do it again and again as the wind continued to strengthen and at its peak, you were diving to the water, skimming four feet above the sharp whitecaps at one hundred and thirty miles an hour, pausing lovely seconds over the water, then zooming up 300 feet to the top where again the lift buoyed the ship back to altitude. Five hours over the cliff; five hours in paradise, watching the other sailplanes in the air and watching the light on the shining ocean change to the deep, harvest yellow of late afternoon.

Every pilot has a special place in his heart for those landings away from home, at the end of a long day in the air. Tucson: a cold night in early spring after being up nearly seven hours, after the save at Redrock when you were less than 500 feet off the ground, then getting back up, struggling all day against a stiff headwind, then at last getting the evening thermal over the city and being a mile high when the sun went down, landing just at dark between runway lights, and being met by the car and trailer driven by Marcel and Bertha Godinat. During the later hours aloft the knees had soaked up cold and at first after getting out it was not possible to walk. Santa Rosa, New Mexico, under a dark overcast pierced by lightning after a hard cross-country day: The thunderstorm had reversed the prevailing airflow and the landing was made downwind in an explosion of elkhorn cactus that flew over wings and canopy. Durango: After a flight across Monument Valley, Cortez, and Hesperus Peak. The field was only two miles short of the airport — a big field, but a new fairing robbed the wheel of its braking power and the ship quit rolling only thirty feet short of the fence. Eight miles west of Aguila: A first attempt to bring in the car and trailer was stopped by fences and a flood control ditch ten feet deep. The second trip was after dark, aided by two pages of handwritten instructions on where to turn, which gates to open, distances, direction, and landmarks. We found the ship and derigged by flashlight. The return, like the entry, was dead-slow, under ten miles per hour, to keep from hitting the nearly invisible Black Angus cows — going back through the same stretched gates of barbed wire, past the night-sound of engine-driven irrigation well pumps, under a brilliant canopy of stars.

The excitement and bustle of a National Soaring Contest! Around the retrieve cars and sailplanes tied down on the line, there are chests of equipment, tool boxes, radios, wingtip stands, oxygen masks, wash buckets and chamois, the smell of camphor used for smoking barograph drums, jackets, parachutes, ice chests, brightly colored canopies of canvas. Inside the hangar, after breakfast, on the pilot meeting tables, you saw briefcases, plastic rulers, marked air charts, tow tickets, landing cards, and note pads. Up near the podium, where the competition director stands, are the weather charts, turnpoint photographs, the painted diagrams of the field showing the staging areas, tiedown apron, and the start gate location. By late morning there were heat waves rising off the concrete apron. Tar expansion joints turned sticky-soft in the sun. A biplane used for towing was parked on the ramp, the shade of its lower wing filled with seated figures watching the takeoffs.

On the third day of the contest there were no clouds but there was an odd haze in the sky, as if the blue had been thickened by flour. Everyone was keeping a sharp eye out for turning sailplanes. As I was rising in the thermal, I began to spot one ship after another, high above me, and when a few more minutes had gone by, other sailplanes joined me down below as we all scaled the invisible ladder of air.

That year many taut contest hours were spent scratching on the deck, beginning with zero sink at four hundred feet, balancing airspeed against faint bursts of lift; down to three hundred and fifty feet, four hundred feet again, three hundred and eighty — circling and circling with despair following hope, above an unterraced field of open plow where the shadow of your sailplane circles with you in a slow duet, a shadow close below, crisp and hard, like the shadow that comes up to meet you during landing — with your chest pulled tight and sweat running freely into soggy clothes. Then slowly, ever so slowly, like a child's balloon that has had most of the gas leak out overnight, the climb begins: 412 feet, 460, 490, 520 — each time the altimeter is tapped with fingertips to get the highest possible reading; and in twenty-five minutes you are up at nine thousand feet where you can relax, breathe, and take out your canteen for a drink.

After a Nebraska landing: The country road you walked out seemed lightly travelled because the tracks of birds and small animals crossed in a number of places and had been put there since the most recent passage of a car. The silence was intense. After some time growing accustomed to it, the void began to fill with the distant hum of insects. Now and again you would be startled by the explosive flight of a pheasant which would burst out of a thicket alongside the road and fly powerfully for a few seconds, never getting over eight feet high, then just as quickly starting a glide which would bring it to earth just beyond shotgun range.

On the open day I did not get lift following my initial tow. When I was down to six hundred feet, there were scraps of rising air, but after a brief struggle I landed at the airport. There was an hour of delay waiting for a new tow, an hour when those in the air were building distance points. The second flight went much the same except that the bits of lift I found came at four hundred feet. Another landing at the field; another delay of forty minutes.

On the third flight I was determined to head out on course, even if it meant accomplishing nothing but a straight glide down to the ground. And straight glide it was — never a bump of lift from the time of release. I saved only enough altitude for a base leg, then turned final and landed in a plowed field, facing into the hot south wind.

I got out of the ship and looked at the horizon, shimmering with heat. There was a nightmare feeling of unreality in being down on the ground at 2:30 in the afternoon, knowing the day was already over. It was one of those blistering afternoons when it seemed impossible to get enough water from your canteen, that made you very careful when touching bare metal that had been left in the sun.

It took an hour to get together with my crew and when we derigged nobody had much to say. It was well after four o'clock when we started for home, but even at that late hour we saw one sailplane being towed aloft for a new flight. He got into the air at 4:22 P. M. and during our brief drive home we could see him circling over the field. He climbed to about three thousand feet and headed west.

We got back to the field at twenty minutes until five, completely beaten. After getting a cold drink at the food stand, I wandered over to the scoreboard, mounted under the wide shade of a tree, where the burning afternoon heat was just now starting to cool.

On such days the world hears about the great flights. Graham Thomson, 195.5 miles north; Wally Scott, 188.5 miles northeast; Dick Johnson, 273 miles, clear up into South Dakota; A. J. Smith, 282 miles, down near Felt, Oklahoma; George Moffat, 277 miles; and Bill Ivans, 216 miles.

On the scoreboard, written in chalk, was the story of those who also flew:

Allemann — Down	Coder — Down — crew is out
May — Gone Home	Emons — Down — no word from crew
Lincoln — Down — Crew there — back to field	Gerste — Down
Gehrlein — Down	Chase — Down
Greene — Down	Karlovich — Down
Derujinsky — Down — crew is out	Bierens — Down — with crew
Schreder — Down — no word from crew	Slacks — Down
Beebe — Down — crew is out	Ryan — Down
Brown — New start 4:22 P. M.	Mozer — Down
Pallmer — Down	Brittingham — Down and back

Contest failures leave wounds that are slow to heal. Those gathered around the scoreboard were back from incredibly short flights. They made quiet talk of other soaring days and put up a brave effort to be cheerful and carefree.

At five o'clock the siren blew. It was the official contest signal that the flight line was closed, and that there could be no more starts. It was an unbelievably mournful sound, a plaint that might have signified eternal defeat.

A happier time: The race north from McCook on a day made for soaring. From time to time in the far distance there would be a flash of sunlight on the wings of a sailplane and you could see one of your fellow pilots turning in a thermal. When he straightened on course, the aircraft would disappear from sight. It was in the harvest season and both on roads and in the wheatfields there were combines on the move. Half the country was cultivated and half was broken virgin soil, warm under the early afternoon sun. All but the main roads had been scraped out of the black earth, and these little country byways ran straight except where they dropped into a creek bed where they wandered about, often passing through a woods near the water. The newly-plowed fields gleamed with the rich black soil of Nebraska; freshly harvested wheatfields were shimmering in the sunlight and near the edge of creeks, the terraced cornfields were intense green. All this color faded as your eye rose toward the distance. The horizon was as firm and even as seascape — it fused together with the sky at what appeared to be the outer edge of the world.

The banquet ending the 1964 National at McCook was very festive. During the speeches and presentation of awards, there was the shared friendship of the sky, a bond very close among soaring pilots. Then suddenly it was all over. People got up from the tables and broke into groups to talk. The National at McCook was gone and the racking emotional letdown at the end of a great contest began — that feeling of irreplaceable loss, when remembering both the good flights and the failures: early afternoon landings and tying down in the blistering yellow heat of midday; the backbreak of hauling a sailplane to the edge of soft-plowed fields; lifting wings gingerly over a barbed wire fence. The Fourth of July beer bust with watermelon, out on the concrete ramp near the main hangar in the cool of early evening, with boys exploding firecrackers around everybody's feet. That was all past now. So was the National at Odessa and the beer party that Al Backstrom had started in my room on the day when the front finally arrived and rain had wiped out contest flying. The motel room was very crowded, with people sitting on the bed, chairs and the floor. Bill Ivans came and played his recorder; Philip Wills was there, sitting on the floor with his knees drawn up, filling his pipe with loving care, then sealing in the tobacco with tiny balls of wadded toilet paper.

My flight to Variadero was over and the Diamond flights and the National at Bishop and the National at Elmira where I first had *Cirro-Q*, my 1–23D, and the National at Grand Prairie, flown open-cockpit in a Baby Albatross. Gone was that early day when I first joined a hawk circling in the crisp air of late morning; the time of first looking down on sailplanes wheeling below me in a thermal over the warm earth, dappled in cloudshadow; and that long ago, late afternoon flight, slowly climbing up toward a gigantic towering cumulus, its knobs in varied shades of a satiny pearl gray except for the west side where it glowed orange-pink facing the low sun — shad-

xviii

ows below growing long, reaching for the horizon, and I knew I would still be aloft when convection stopped, and would glide down through golden quiet air.

Every pilot, if he has striven long enough, has had nightmare cross-country flights which ended in bad landings. All day long the sink was murderous; thermals were torn up by the wind, the sky was full of holes, and each climb seemed likely to be the last. And now, low above hostile country, the landing was going to be a choice between that sandy river bottom, the rough plateau country beyond, or the road, booby trapped with marker posts.

Breathing grew erratic as you watched the trembling dance of the variometer needle; belly muscles tightened and sweat ran down your side from armpits even though the cockpit was cool. You strained to hear the rising whine of the Crossfell electric variometer, which could mean a save; legs ached because for minutes they had been tensed.

The final approach was to a short field, beyond a road, with the wind direction misjudged and control falling away at the moment of touchdown. A violent ground-loop made the left wingtip cut a great scimitar stroke into powdered-sugar dust, throwing up a tiny cloud which was instantly carried off by the wind. In the heart, sickening self-reproach at the damage caused to the sailplane — feeling as you would feel if you had brutalized a child or a helpless animal.

An increasing number of pilots have experienced flight in the mountain wave. The cold weather kit for wave flying! Base layer is cotton thermal underwear with thermal socks, over which go two pairs of cashmere socks and finally heavy wool socks with electric heating elements. The second layer is a heavy cotton shirt and thick wool flannel trousers. Then a loose wool shirt and the green windbreaker jacket of nylon. The outer layer is an Eddie Bauer quilted goosedown jacket and trousers, goosedown gloves, a soft helmet, and sheepskin-lined boots of the type used by the bomber crews of World War II at high altitude.

In the sailplane is a pressure-breathing oxygen mask, the parachute with a bail-out oxygen bottle which is tied into a heavy canvas pouch, the usual seat belt, shoulder harness, and a light blanket to put over your legs.

At 30,000 feet it is twenty Fahrenheit degrees below zero in the cockpit. There is a chilling breeze which could quick-freeze meat, but the body is warm even though the air vents are open to prevent breath condensation snow from forming on the inside of the plexiglass canopy. No snow does form, just a delicate spiderweb tracery of frost.

Far below is an undercast of wooly cloud, gleaming in the late afternoon sun, solid from horizon to horizon except for the opening and closing wave windows straight down, blinking between earth and sky with glacial slowness.

Down in that other world — the dark earth-world from where you took off — it has been snowing all afternoon.

On a record flying expedition there were the days when we got up in the morning to see the sky covered with the hated, oppressive white glare of cirro-stratus overcast. We flew anyway, but the soaring was difficult, as if the air crushed the earth with insupportable dead weight, and the few thin dust devils were too feeble to push it away.

After all the failures and useless retrieves, after the times when the weather forecast went sour, when the meterorologist called a nearly cloudless day with strong thermals and you were shot down by snow flurries and a heavy overcast which had blown out of a massive thunderhead; after all of this came the landing at Jack Gallette's Fly-in Ranch, just south of Santa Fe. We had been aloft nine and a half hours and had flown a world record over the whole length of the Sangre de Cristo Mountains.

We were aloft in the bright morning air, catching the early, toddling, unsure thermals, then mounting toward the high ridge, past the narrow fields on the western slope, past the tender groves of aspen, soaring beyond the ancient village of Taos, pressing ever northward.

At Alamosa the Rio Grande has no canyon as it does farther down. It meanders lazily southward across the high plain of the San Luis Valley, as if regretting it must leave at all. In the near distance to the east is Blanca Peak, the slopes with a strong upward thrust, mounting without a break toward the snow-covered summits which have patches of dark rock showing through the soft white blanket. That is Blanca Peak as the landsman sees it. The airman sees a very different mountain looking down from 18,000 feet. He sees a group of cirques radiating outward from the central mass. High on the western side, in the tight valley bottom of a cirque, there is a tiny lake; and ahead, on the ground to the north, lies the Great Sand Dunes National Monument with dunes up to 700 feet high, but from this altitude they are the coarse ripples of a beach, passing under your feet on a windy afternoon.

We flew on, clear to Salida, Colorado, the turnpoint, where we photographed the airport; then we started home, tiptoeing through the cirrus overcast the first thirty miles of the way back, almost going down near Fort Garland and once again by Taos, but the day kept faith. In late afternoon we climbed up to cloudbase a final time.

South of Truches Peak in the lower Sangre de Cristo Mountains there are a number of tiny lakes, frozen over even in late spring. Parts of the ice have the color of liquid turquoise — that hot, coppery, desert blue, completely incongruous in those foreboding, windswept heights above timberline, but lovely past description at this moment, within gliding range of our goal.

xx

The landing was after sunset, with light growing purple and soft. Afterward, the congratulations of the party who had gathered to see us in, drinking champagne the host had provided while daylight was fading from the western horizon. And like a song inside the chest was that luminous warm glow of achievement.

This is something of what one man has found in soaring over a span of seventeen years which have seen a thousand hours aloft in sailplanes. There have been endless retrieves, journeys across the Continent on the way to competitions, and the soaring talk on long winter nights while awaiting springtime when once again the hawk will fly, and dust devils are the harbinger of thermals and cumulus clouds.

The main part of this book tries to show a glimpse of flight through the words of other writers and soaring photographers.

JOSEPH COLVILLE LINCOLN

A Schweizer 1–23 on winch tow above Torrey Pines. GEORGE UVEGES

*Six or seven meters velocity of wind, suffice to enable
the sailing surface of eighteen square meters to carry me
almost horizontally against the wind from the top
of my hill without any starting jump. If the wind is
stronger, I allow myself to be simply lifted from
the point of the hill and sail slowly toward the wind. The
direction of the flight has, in strong winds, a strong
upward tendency. I often reach positions in the air which
are much higher than my starting point.*

OTTO LILIENTHAL

Otto Lilienthal preparing to launch his 1895 biplane hang-glider
from the point of his artificial hill. SMITHSONIAN INSTITUTION

Before take-off, a professional pilot is keen, anxious,
but lest someone read his true feelings, he is elaborately
casual. The reason for this is that he is about to enter
a new though familiar world. The process of entrance
begins a short time before he leaves the ground and is
completed the instant he is in the air. From that moment
on, not only his body but his spirit and personality
exist in a separate world known only to himself and
his comrades.

As the years go by he returns to this invisible world
rather than to earth for peace and solace. There he also
finds a profound enchantment although he can seldom
describe it. He can discuss it with others of his kind, and
because they, too, know and feel its power they under-
stand. But his attempts to communicate his feelings to his
wife or other earthly confidants invariably end in
failure. Flying is hypnotic and all pilots are willing vic-
tims to the spell. Their world is like a magic island . . .

ERNEST K. GANN

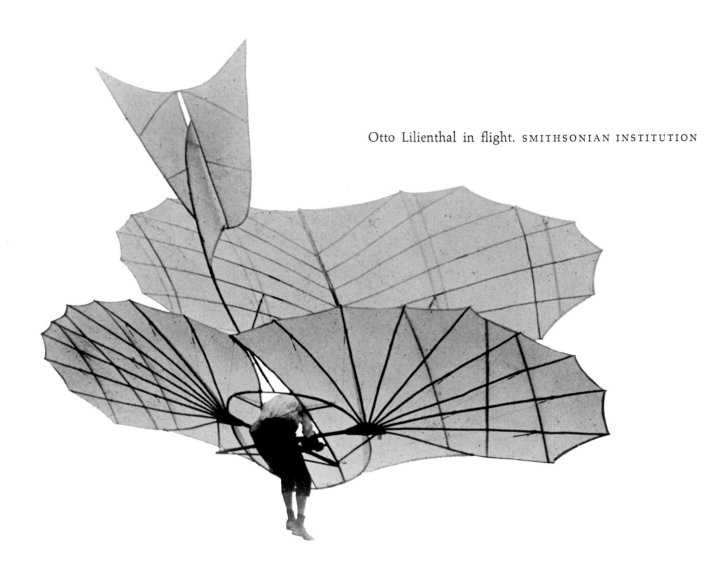

Otto Lilienthal in flight. SMITHSONIAN INSTITUTION

5

. . . the chilly December day
two shivering bicycle mechanics from Dayton, Ohio,
first felt their homemade contraption
whittled out of hickory sticks,
gummed together with Arnstein's bicycle cement,
stretched with muslin they'd sewn on their sister's
sewing machine in their own backyard on Hawthorn
Street in Dayton, Ohio,
soar into the air
above the dunes and the wide beach
at Kitty Hawk.

JOHN DOS PASSOS

6

1902. The Wright brothers at Big Kill Devil Hill. WRIGHT BROTHERS PAPERS

1921. Shockcord launching the first sailplane, the Hanover *Vampyr*. RICHARD MILLER COLLECTION

The Platz Canard of 1923. PETER M. BOWERS COLLECTION

I saw the heather bow and crush beneath the skid. . . .
Faster and faster, till I knew that if I pulled back on the
stick I should fly. Gently I pressed back — oh, so
gently — and then without any warning the earth and
I parted company. I was flying — flying! I wanted to
shout it to the heavens.

TERENCE HORSLEY

9

Oh! I have slipped the surly bonds of earth
And danced the skies on laughter-silvered wings;
Sunward I've climbed, and joined the tumbling mirth
of sun-split clouds — and done a hundred things
You have not dreamed of—wheeled and soared and swung
High in the sunlit silence. Hov'ring there,
I've chased the shouting wind along, and flung
My eager craft through footless halls of air.

Up, up, the long delirious burning blue
I've topped the wind-swept heights with easy grace
Where never lark or even eagle flew—
And, while with silent lifting mind I've trod
The high untrespassed sanctity of space,
Put out my hand and touched the face of God.

JOHN GILLESPIE MAGEE, JR.

World Record pilot, Wallace A. Scott, in his AS–W 12. SANDOR A. ALDOTT

10

Cherokee. ALLEN A. DUTTON

*Their slim shapes are smooth to touch and slippery
like ice. Their rounded backs catch the light and reflect
it like polished glass. Their curves are symmetrical,
continuous, and blended into one another as geometrical
designs which are happily married. When their wings
are against the sky they are transparent, and you can see
their ribs against the light beyond. No bird had
better-shaped wings, no wings were ever spread in such
a challenge. To see them is to know they can fly—
that they belong to the wind and the sky and that they
are part of it as much as the clouds of a summer day.*

TERENCE HORSLEY

12

Pratt-Read. ALLEN A. DUTTON

Schweizer 1–24. ALLEN A. DUTTON

Wave cloud over Boulder, Colorado. JOHN ARMITAGE

Subtle hints of the waning day were coming my way
each time the ship turned in the process of thermaling.
Somewhere in the front cowl, a small hole was casting
a white spot of sunlight which earlier in the day had
marched across my legs and up behind the instrument
panel. Now it was sweeping across my lap with each
rotation and was accompanied by the dark passage
of the high wing shadow flashing through the cockpit
each time the wing blocked the sinking sun from view.

KENNETH H. ARTERBURN, JR.

16

An Austria watches the sunset. GEORGE UVEGES

Tail view of a Foka. GEORGE UVEGES

Open end of an oval trailer. GEORGE UVEGES

Libelle: nose, canopy, and towrope. GEORGE UVEGES

Ladder to the sky; an uncovered LK wing. ALLEN A. DUTTON

And this, the air, has also been your schooling. Now
you will know by the feel how it thins and expands in
summer, losing its buoyancy, and how in winter
when around the windscreen and your goggles the slip-
stream bites to the cheekbone. You have learned the
clouds, line squalls, cold fronts, stratus, the slaty cirrus;
alto-cumulus in white plough-furrows; cumulonimbus
piling up through the troposphere, enclosing in billowy,
mountainous chimney bellowing updraughts.

FLEMING MacLIESH

The Polish Foka. GEORGE UVEGES

22

Briegleb BG–12. GEORGE UVEGES

Anne Morrow Lindbergh, from *North to the Orient*, copyright, 1935, 1963, reprinted by permission of Harcourt Brace Jovanovich, Inc.

Dark — that curfew hour in a flier's mind, when
the gates are closed, the portcullis dropped down, and
there is no way to go around or to squeeze under
the bars if one is late.

But now, seeing signs of approaching night — the
coves and lagoons took up the light the sky was losing –
I was afraid. I felt the terror of a savage seeing a first
eclipse, or even as if I had never known night.

The shadow of a wing covered all the sky. We would
be covered, inclosed, crushed. Wisps of evening fog
below grew luminous in the approaching dark. I remem-
bered now what night was. It was being blind and
lost and trapped. It was looking and not seeing — that
was night.

ANNE MORROW LINDBERGH

A parade of American world record sailplanes
flying near Marfa, Texas. From left: The Sisu–1A
built by Leonard A. Niemi, the HP–8 by
Richard E. Schreder, and the R–6 by Harland C. Ross.
SANDOR A. ALDOTT

A Diamant banking near Calistoga, California. JOHN ARMITAGE, CHARLES A. HILL, JR.

29

*I stood fascinated while he drifted down, swinging
with the wind, a part of it, the 'chute's skirt weaving
with its eddies, lightly, gracefully, until he struck
the ground and all that fragile beauty wilted around
him into a pile of earth-stained, wrinkled cloth.*

CHARLES A. LINDBERGH

Edward Makula, Polish World Champion and Lilienthal Medal winner. GEORGE UVEGES

30

Richard H. Johnson, seven times National Soaring
Champion, with his wife Alice. E. J. REEVES

Father and son, with Alice Johnson and Nels. ALLEN A. DUTTON

Interior of a sailplane trailer equipped with a top that raises up on hinged legs. ALLEN A. DUTTON

A Cirrus wing being lifted out of its trailer at Marfa, Texas. ALLEN A. DUTTON

*The air to a glider pilot is a reality, not a shadow
on a screen. He is in direct relationship with it, he is
trying to understand it in all its moods; to learn
its flow, its laws, and to try and use this knowledge to
his own ends.... The air is vast, sometimes strange
and gray and lonely, but also it can laugh and play in all
the colours of the rainbow; it can be friendly and
it has its own intimacies.*

PHILIP A. WILLS

ALDO PANZIERI

*In dreams, I often had the feeling that I was stalling
— that unmistakable feeling that you get when you slow
up an airplane beyond the critical point. When the
wings lose their grip on the air and begin to feel like legs
that have gone to sleep, numb and useless, and then
they buckle — not actually, but it feels as if they did,
and the ship falls off forward and unless there is altitude
below you, it falls onto the ground.*

WOLFGANG LANGEWIESCHE

36

It is appearance, characteristics and performance
that make a man love an airplane, and they, told truly,
are what put the emotion into one.
  You love a lot of things if you live around them,
but there isn't any woman and there isn't any horse,
nor any before nor any after, that is as lovely as a
great airplane, and men who love them are faithful to
them even though they leave them for others.

ERNEST HEMINGWAY

Speed! Wallace A. Scott flying an AS–W 12 near Marfa, Texas. SANDOR A. ALDOTT

Following two pages: Searching for the best lift beyond an overcast. Sumner Davis piloting his 2–32. JOHN ARMITAGE

Preceding two pages: Searching for a hole
in solid valley undercast. JOHN ARMITAGE

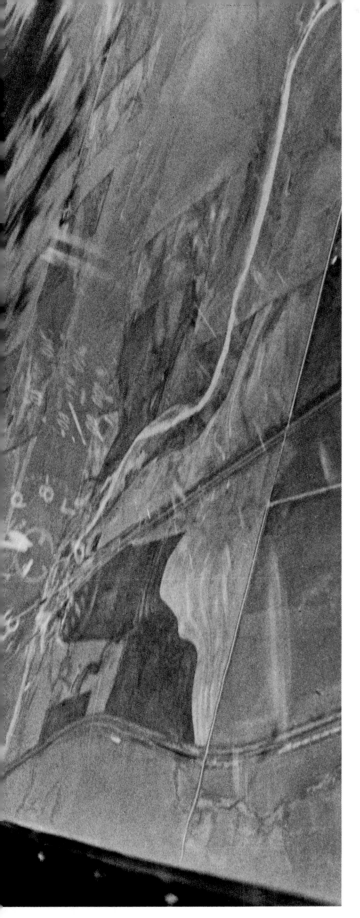

I am tensely watching the mottled blur of mesquite,
sage, and sand speeding below when without warning
I reel from a bone-grinding jar that combines with
a piteous groan from the sailplane's innards. Before I can
even consider a midair, the ship is lurching, skidding,
and twisting in all directions. I am in a maelstrom of
turbulence. Its blows are abrupt, shattering,
instantaneous. Most frightening of all are moments when
outside sound stops. The sudden quiet in the cockpit
is so hushed I can hear the barograph ticking. My own
innards spasm to zero-gravity. I'm falling!

DOUGLAS LAMONT

Pilot's eye view of the horizon and cloudbase while in a right bank of 60 degrees. JOHN ARMITAGE

45

Two Schweizer 1–23s fly a duet between field and cloud. ROBERT LEE MOORE

46

And a pair of TG–3s approach cloudbase over the desert near El Mirage. PAUL W. HEASLEY

Ivory Tower! A Schweizer 1–21
and a BG–12 anticipate a great day
of soaring. ROBERT LEE MOORE

49

The two-seater sailplane of those days was a crude machine. It had a square, fabric-covered fuselage, while a single high wing was supported on struts. I took the rear seat. Then in a moment a flag dropped and the cable tightened. We were snatched into the air after a few bumpy yards on the skid, and were climbing steeply like a kite hauled into the teeth of the wind. Four hundred yards away a winch was reeling up the wire, but all that I could see was the sky, and all that I heard was the flute-like noise of the wind in the rigging and the creak of timber as the fuselage absorbed the tractive power of the cable.

We were free, poised in almost perfect silence. . . . We climbed from 400 to 2,000 feet in a few minutes, wafted through a veil of liquid gold towards the west. Once we passed close to another craft, from which the pilot gave us a great shout of greeting. So might two gods have called to each other from their kingdoms.

TERENCE HORSLEY

50

Hooking up a 2–22 for winch launch at Torrey Pines, California. ALLEN A. DUTTON

Airplane tows carry you out over the sea. ALLEN A. DUTTON

Going aloft on winch tow. ALLEN A. DUTTON

53

The Torrey Pines winch. Driver sits in a protective cage of steel netting. ALLEN A. DUTTON

Two Schweizer 1-26s work ridge lift above the cliff. ROSE MARIE LICHER

Champions. Richard E. Schreder in his HP–8 flies in formation with A. J. Smith in his LO–150. JOHN D. RYAN

A Bowlus Super-Albatross cruising above the surf. DON DOWNIE

Of course there is beauty in soaring. But in the Championships you fly to beat people, not for contemplation. The Championships are brutal: brutal to nature, brutal on the ships, brutal on the pilots . . .

GLEB DERUJINSKY

58

This trainer has landed on the beach, but will soon be retrieved by aerotow. ALLEN A. DUTTON

The unmistakable creamy smooth lift showed that wave-lift was about. This was it: I swung smoothly round into wind and hung almost stationary in space climbing silkily upwards. Overhead was a flat and rather dirty sheet of cloud, stretching as far as I could see in all directions. I found myself rising with gently increasing speed towards it, until in a short time it quietly took me in. The lift increased further and quite suddenly I burst forth into a scene that might have been on another planet.

I was flying north along the eastern slope of a gigantic, an endless, valley of dazzling cloud. The sun, which we had not seen for over a week, was blazing down from a sky of cloudless dark blue, striking from the rounded walls and floor of the cloud valley a white and insupportable glare.

The scene had the stark and splendid geometrical simplicity of a certain kind of nightmare. The cloud valley ran straight as a ruler ahead of me as far as the eye could reach. I was flying along in almost utter silence, with my right wing nearly touching the eastern slope, and about a third of the way up towards its crest, climbing steadily.

PHILIP A. WILLS

A boomerang window in the wave over Bishop, California. WARREN WATSON

60

Lenticular wave clouds near Boulder, Colorado. JOHN ARMITAGE

Meanwhile the Adversary of God and Man,
Satan with thought inflam'd of highest design,
Puts on swift wings, and toward the Gates of Hell
Explores his solitary flight: sometimes
He scours the right hand coast, sometimes the left;
Now shaves with level wing the Deep, then soares
Up to the fiery concave towering high.

Into the wilde Expanse, and through the shock
Of fighting Elements, on all sides round
Environ'd, wins his way.

JOHN MILTON

64

Athens, new and old. A wave cloud over the Acropolis. SANDOR A. ALDOTT

Angel flight. Waves in the lee of Mount Rainier. PAUL W. HEASLEY

Bishop, California. A giant west foehn wind pitches headlong down the Sierra Nevada. ROBERT SYMONS

67

68   A lenticular cloud stretching southward from Boulder, Colorado. JOHN ARMITAGE

. . . He had flown the mail with Lindbergh on Robertson Airlines. As he spoke, his strangely delicate hands flew graceful little glides, dives, and chandelles, and his face came alive as can only a man's who is totally in love.

ERNEST K. GANN

The upper Sangre de Cristo mountain range, looking north from 24,000 feet. JOHN ARMITAGE

The men and their machines are both transient and fragile: The granite of the mountain will outlast all but their spirit.

BENNETT M. ROGERS

Soaring along the Dragontail Mountains. RUDOLPH T. ALLEMANN

An Orlik sailplane on airtow over Bishop, California. ROBERT SYMONS

71

Gull winged Orlik soaring in the wave near the California Sierra. ROBERT SYMONS

My fingers are numbed by the cold. Muscles, nerves, and marrow finally begin shaking in revolt. Yet I smile inwardly. Here is a blob of quivering human flesh, restrained by straps in deep-freeze, barbecued with ultra-violet radiation, impaled on the skewer of its own backbone, then jammed into a tiny cocoon of exquisite shape, the whole hung suspended four miles above the earth in a realm of deep blue serenity. I can stand apart from physical travail and contemplate the sight below.

The entire Sierra wall lies stretched ahead, a spindrift of snowy rock from the west, arrested in time at the moment it washes upon the beach of the desert. A still-brilliant sun at my right wing-tip faces down the full moon rising at my left. The sail-plane and I are a procession of one, passing through an immense corridor between celestial dignitaries.

I am supremely happy. This must be what they call nirvana.

DOUGLAS LAMONT

It was a pale incorporeal wind that seemed to penetrate the earth and every breathing thing upon the face of the earth — blowing as it has blown through all memory and song.

GUY MURCHIE

Wave soaring the Orlik. ROBERT SYMONS

75

Exaltation! Paul F. Bikle maneuvers his 1-23 near a Sierran pinnacle. ROBERT SYMONS

Cecil M. Craig making a winter cross-country flight down the Cascade Range. JIM LARSEN

Looking down on the summit of Pike's Peak from 24,000 feet. JOHN ARMITAGE

78

Following two pages: The Colorado Massif, from 14,000 feet. JOHN ARMITAGE

The familiar airstream noise turned to a gentle whisper, indicating that the smooth streamline of the wave had encircled the airframe. The door to the upper sky had opened.

At 24,500, still rising at 50 feet per minute, the ship flew into a vaporous envelope containing millions of tiny silver needles. Hanging there suspended without power in a translucent cloud of delicate ice crystals produced an eerie feeling of loneliness. It was as if the world had been left behind and I had passed into a Shangri-la where dreams were transmuted into realities. A foretaste of the Elysian Fields...

EDWARD P. WILLIAMS

A Diamant soaring in the Mount St. Helena wave. JOHN ARMITAGE

Intuition and instinct, so dormant during most of our soaring hours, play the most vital role in such dramatic saves. When the perspiration is trickling down between my back and my parachute, my knuckles are protruding like white bones on the backs of my hands, and I am talking aloud to myself as I realize, with a sinking heart, that I can distinguish the separate leaves on the trees underneath — in times like these I have often felt an impulse to gamble my few remaining feet of altitude to fly off in a new direction; something tells me, there will be lift. And more often than not, thank God, there is.

GRENVILLE SEIBELS, II

A Libelle circling in a thermal above the Sawtooth range. ROBERT LEE MOORE

Aerotowing on a lazy Sunday afternoon. ALDO PANZIERI

A Schweizer 1–23G makes a speed run over Odessa. SANDOR A. ALDOTT

86

Even while looking over at the aeroplane's shadow running prettily over land and sea, I had the impression of extreme slowness. Within the rigid spread of the powerful planes, I had sometimes the illusion of sitting as if by enchantment in a block of suspended marble.

JOSEPH CONRAD

88

A Kestrel pulls up, just after passing through the
finish gate at the end of a speed task. ALLEN A. DUTTON

An Austria soars over the field at McCook, Nebraska. GEORGE UVEGES

A Libelle coming home after a day of wave
soaring near Pike's Peak. SANDOR A. ALDOTT

91

Antoine de Saint-Exupéry, from "The Elements" in *Wind, Sand and Stars,*
by permission of Harcourt Brace Jovanovich, Inc., New York.

I had taken off from the field at Trelew and was
flying down to Comodoro-Rivadavia, in the Patagonian
Argentine. Here the crust of the earth is as dented
as an old boiler. The sky was blue. A hard blue sky that
shone over the scraped and barren world while
the fleshless vertebrae of the mountain chain flashed
in the sunlight.

ANTOINE DE SAINT-EXUPÉRY

92

Over the Sawtooth Range. ROBERT LEE MOORE

Searching for any kind of lift, far below the summit. ROBERT LEE MOORE

94

Getting low above hostile terrain, the Joshua sentineled Mojave. ALDO PANZIERI

Local soaring on a hazy afternoon. ALLEN A. DUTTON

Late afternoon. The pilot studies earth and sky, looking for signs of lift which will prolong his flight. JOHN ARMITAGE

Turning on final approach for landing in a smooth field of stubble. JOHN ARMITAGE

Following two pages: A Schweizer 2–32
after landing on a mesa. JOHN ARMITAGE

When we had first commenced our flight, I was appalled by the manner in which we can take the miraculous for granted. . . .

There was a curious distortion of perception. Even at the lower altitudes it had been very difficult to judge height, distance — even attitude and direction. Now the effect was multiplied. There was no sensation of flight or motion. Once denied motion, it is impossible to hang onto time. So there you are — suspended, motionless, alone in a timeless sky transfixed by an overwhelming sun that burns only for you.

GUY GOSSELIN

Twenty-four thousand feet high in the Sangre de Cristo Wave. JOHN ARMITAGE

Acknowledgments

The editor wishes to express his thanks to the following photographers for permission to use their fine work which appears on the listed pages:

ii, 1, 17, 18, 19, 20, 22, 23, 31, 37, 89   George Uveges

3, 5   Smithsonian Institution

6, 7   Wright Brothers, from *The Papers of Wilbur and Orville Wright,*
    edited by Marvin W. McFarland, McGraw-Hill Book Company, Inc.

8   Peter M. Bowers Collection

9   Richard Miller Collection

11, 26-27, 39, 64, 87, 90-91   Sandor A. Aldott (one-time rights)

12, 13, 21, 24, 33, 34, 35, 51, 52, 53, 54, 58-59, 88, 95   Allen A. Dutton

14-15   John Armitage

28   John Armitage and Charles A. Hill, Jr.

40-41, 42-43, 44, 62-63, 68, 69, 78-79 , 80-81, 82-83, 96, 97, 98-99, 101   John Armitage

29   Gleb Derujinsky

32   E. J. Reeves

36, 86, 94   Aldo Panzieri

46, 48-49, 85, 92, 93   Robert Lee Moore

47, 65   Paul W. Heasley

55   Rose Marie Licher

56   Don Downie

57   John D. Ryan

61   Warren Watson

66-67, 70, 72, 74-75, 76   Robert Symons

71   Rudolph T. Allemann

77   Jim Larsen

The editor also expresses his gratitude to the following individuals and publishers for permission to include selections of their work which is credited and listed by page:

vii, 30   Charles A. Lindbergh, *The Spirit of St. Louis*, by permission of Charles Scribner's Sons, New York.

2   Otto Lilienthal, from the book *The Book of Gliders* by Edwin Way Teale, Copyright 1930 by E. P. Dutton & Co., Inc. Renewal © 1958 by Edwin Way Teale. Published by E. P. Dutton & Co., Inc., and used with their permission.

4   Ernest K. Gann, *Island in the Sky*, by permission of Ernest K. Gann.

69   Ernest K. Gann, from *Fate is the Hunter*, permission by Simon & Schuster, Inc., New York, 1961.

6   John Dos Passos, from "The Campers at Kitty Hawk," copyright by H. Marston Smith and Elizabeth H. Dos Passos, co-executors of the estate of John Dos Passos, by permission of the co-executors.

9, 12, 50   Terence Horsley, from *Soaring Flight*, by permission of Eyre & Spottiswoode (Publishers), Ltd., London.

10   John Gillespie Magee, Jr., poem "High Flight" by permission of Mrs. John G. Magee and David B. Magee

16   Kenneth H. Arterburn, Jr., from "Diamonds at Eagle Pass," *Soaring* Magazine, January 1969, by permission of the author.

22   Fleming MacLiesh, from "Exploration by Air," in *The Poetry of Flight*, Books for Libraries, reprint edition, by permission of Hawthorn Books, Inc.

35, 60   Philip A. Wills, from *The Beauty of Gliding*, Pitman Publishing Company, London, by permission of the author.

36   Wolfgang Langewiesche, from "Knapsack of Salvation," by permission of the author.

38   Ernest Hemingway, from "London Fights the Robots," *Collier's* Magazine, August 19, 1944.

45, 73   Douglas Lamont, from "Flawed Diamond," *Soaring* Magazine, August, 1969, by permission of the author.

57   Gleb Derujinsky, from page 9 of the September, 1968, issue of *Soaring* Magazine, by permission of the author.

64   John Milton, from *Paradise Lost Book II*.

70   Bennett M. Rogers, from page 10 of the March, 1969, issue of *Soaring* Magazine, by permission of the author.

75   Guy Murchie, from *Song of the Sky*, by permission of Houghton Mifflin Company, Boston.

79   Edward P. Williams, from "In the Hall of the Mountain King" in the December 1968 issue of *Soaring* Magazine.

84   Grenville Seibels II, from *Pilot's Choice*, Soaring Symposia, Cumberland, Maryland, by permission.

88   Joseph Conrad, from *Notes on Life and Letters*, by permission of J. M. Dent & Sons, Ltd. and the Trustees of the Joseph Conrad Estate.

100   Guy Gosselin, from "A Timeless Sky," *Soaring* Magazine, February, 1968.

Finally, I would like to express my thanks to Mary C. Flynn for help on this project from the beginning, Frederic S. Marquardt for editorial suggestions, Bill Flynn for work on the photographic prints, and Robert Jacobson who designed the book.

JOSEPH COLVILLE LINCOLN